ARCH OF
PERSPECTIVE

by Jean Watts

Ohio Psychology

Publishing Company

400 East Town Street

Suite 020

Columbus, Ohio 43215

Published by Ohio Psychology Publishing Company
400 East Town Street, Suite 020, Columbus, Ohio 43215
Copyright, © 1989 by Ohio Psychology Publishing Company.
All rights reserved. This publication, or parts thereof, may not
be reproduced in any form without prior written permission of
the Ohio Psychology Publishing Company.
Printed and bound in the United States of America.

Library of Congress Cataloguing in Publication Data

Watts, Jean
  In Search of Perspective

ISBN 0-910707-14-6

Dedicated to Mum + Dad and my mirthful family
(yes, that includes you).

It was so close — the secret of the universe lay before me. But it was multiple choice. And then I woke up.

Why can't teaching be like playing cards..
You take what you're dealt, but you get
to discard one?

Couldn't we just sign a truce or something?

You have a way of making these lessons quite vivid, ma'am.

So in third period he starts in again — and I said "Euclid — can't you just accept some things on faith?" but no...

Thank you for sharing that with us, Billy.

Wait – just one more minute...
I know he'll do something gifted...

It's ok Miss Wilson, I didn't really want to go to any special classes. I don't mind just you and me having some time alone here.

Think the superintendent will buy it?

I don't think you kids realize how much your mother craves solitude.

I don't know!...she stepped into her new classroom, said "12 bulletin boards," and that was it.

Look Mom! There's Mrs. Beane! She teaches hot lunch!

Good tall potential, but we generally wait for a few developmental milestones.

This student-teacher ratio of 30,000 to 1 makes teaching as I'd like nearly impossible.

By laminating herself she hoped
to last through the year with this class.

I could read fine if I just didn't have to know all these words.

I'm sorry Miss Topsfield, but we must stick to school policy. If we let one of them be a carnivore, we'll have to start letting them all.

I don't think "thwarting their urges" should be included in the goal statements miss Otz.

Mom! Walter's playing evolution with himself again!

As long theorized, on March 8th a new life form began to emerge from Jason's sixth grade desk.

Only a person with no third grade
sympathies could have spelled "ough"
words this way.

I'll have... let's see... some advanced mathematics individually paced, some special ed. spelling... and perhaps just some dittos in social studies...

Perhaps I should aim for control first, then start the lesson.

It's not math anxiety...just give me
a minute...my name will come to me.

It's so hard to cheat when
you're expected to be creative.

Could I ask how your tests are normed?

Isn't that kid about due for a 10,000 word checkup, Barbara?

No, this one should fit my curriculum. It's forty minutes long.

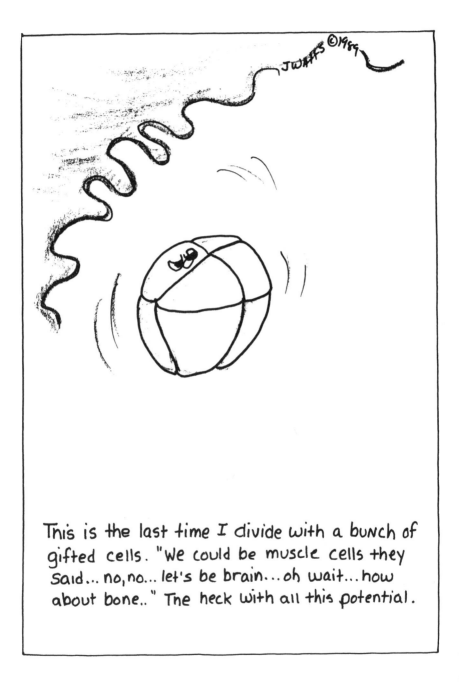

This is the last time I divide with a bunch of
gifted cells. "We could be muscle cells they
said... no, no... let's be brain... oh wait... how
about bone.." The heck with all this potential.

I have a sinking feeling about this IQ test.
I don't see a single question on gear ratios
or carburators.

State of the art IQ tests here – you can save yourselves a lot of trouble if you'll just stand and reveal your giftedness now and get it overwith.

I don't care if you have resolved the great extinction problem...if that room isn't clean in ten minutes you've had it!

Let me get this straight... you want me to stop hanging out, read books for about ten more years so I can impress some people who don't like me now, doing something I never heard of?

Well, how was your first day teaching?

JWAHS © 1988

We understand you have outstanding potential Wayne, but you will have to contribute some effort yourself to benefit from our program.

Now it's time for some probing questions.

How come he always gets to be a muscle cell?

They expect us to believe people wrote with goose feathers? Can you imagine a keyboard made of goosefeathers?

My mother said it isn't feminine to evolve.

I suppose the phrase "A is for Apple"
means nothing to you.

Come on, you can do it... say onomatopoeia...
on..o..mat...o...peeee..ah...

He's either from out of state, or a perfectionist.

Coping is my strength.

Mrs. Moa found keeping a log greatly improved classroom management.

I've mapped out the concepts I've already grasped to save you time.

I'm looking for something that will tell me how I can be totally unique without anyone being able to tell.

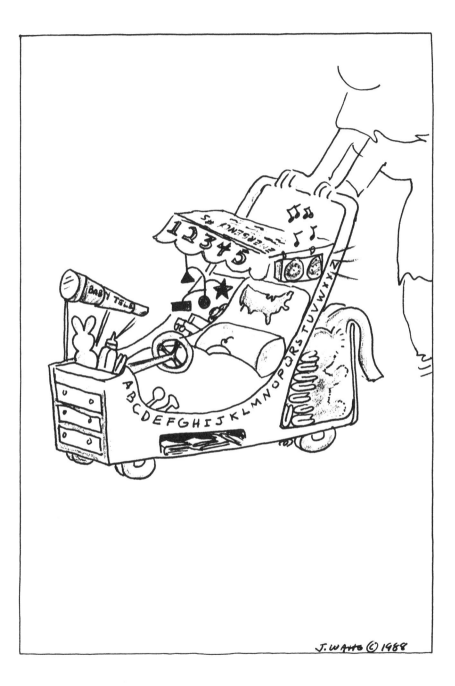

Yes Thor, very good... it does look as if
we are in for a cold snap.

OK... what absurdity juxtaposed with tragedy has occurred to you this time?

I didn't think it was legal to get first year teachers to lead these things.

If I admit to being gifted,

exactly what's in it for me ?

Now let's see, Miss O'Link, you're saying the state insists we add warbling to the curriculum...

I think we could get this if they'd use base one hundred for a change.

I'll tell you one thing. I'd whip them into shape fast. I don't believe in a loose unstructured class at this level.

I think so. Could we take it from the top and try the right brain this time?

And the next time my kid's going to flunk a paper, I want to be told in advance.

Brute strength is fine, but myself, I prefer the creative approach.

This was a terrible assignment. It took me three days to make this for him.

Write what you remember from the
lesson yesterday on the lines below.
Be neat.

JWatts © 1988

What — you never saw a shark
learning frenzy?

The neighbors tried in vain to disprove the "picked it up on his own" theory.

Drat. I can never remember what mnemonic means.

Now that teacher pay has improved, I can spend a lot more on classroom aids.

Back to Basics

If I get the answer right, does that mean you'll like me?

Glow in the dark? What on earth good is
a sundial that glows in the dark?

The wimp mammals got the bullies to meet them ut the tar pits, pulling a major coup

When the state mandated the top 5% as gifted, did they say what they meant by "top"?

See? I knew he started using that Socratic questioning technique for a good reason.

If the year round school idea passes we'll have no time left for any serious learning.

I've put together a few ideas I think she should consider concerning Lillisue's education and how best to deal with her unique behavior.

Where might I find your stabbing and killing books?

Dear, I'm sure she meant "sort of your best," not your absolute best on this assignment.

Not a bad idea to bathe every 6,000 miles at this grade level, Stuart.

Do you have a book about a kid who will kill his sister if she tells on him again?

Mister, that's a relatively inefficient and highly risky means of increasing your capital – if I could suggest...

It's unusual, but she never has any trouble getting their attention.

Fortunately, just as you think you'll go crazy, Mother Nature sends them off blissfully to slumberland.

...and tonight – tune in with millions world wide as we bring you "Hints on Being Creatively Unique."

You finding it difficult
to maintain your aspirations?

The Muskoxen Teachers' Association soon discovered team teaching was the answer to the spitball problem.

According to those Darwin people, she
had ancestors on one of those islands who
have evolved into who knows what by now.
Opportunities for advancement are zero here.

Shhh...now, act innocent...don't let them
know I've filled you in...

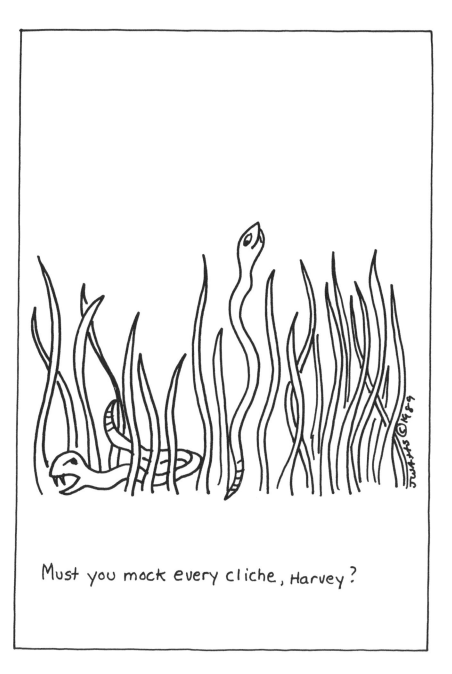

Must you mock every cliche, Harvey?

Clarissa did what she could not to stand out in class.

Yes, I'd say he's gifted... his mother
has tried to give him away several
times — with no success.

By agreeing to your gifted pullout program
ma'am, you understand we are talking about
potential — I do not necessarily include any
set grade point, vocabulary, test scores or
specific graduate school. Nor do I wish
to give up recess.

Solitary was no deterrent for the gifted prisoners, so now we toss them in here.

Mrs. O. found hands-on activities a strain.

Maaaa! Will you make him stop using my toothbrush! You think I want to catch his hiccups?

... and the cloth computer is for my
parents to punch when they're upset.

As long as I respect them as students,
I'm sure they'll be no problem to teach.

For pity's sake, Liza...I'm not going to be able to use those rocks if you keep punching holes in them.

You'd think they'd make kindness an academic subject these days.

How a performance based curriculum might work...

Now, one at a time...jump!

Well, according to tests, she's performing way beyond her ability, so don't expect it to last...

So I thought, why not just do it all the first day and get it over with?

Ms. Plotz' job appeared in jeopardy since most of her students tested below the mean.

Is it my grades? The remark about the
fascist detention policy? What?.. tell me...

I'm not sure. What do you think?
Am I decisive?

Dad, when you were just a seed, did you
know you wanted to be an apple tree?

Mom, I know you and Dad are the Easter Bunny. But how do you get all that candy to all those houses so fast?

I would aspire to a higher level, but they say
the pressure is so low up there its not worth
turning yourself inside out for.

I did too load the dishwasher, but it's Sam's turn to shut the door and add the soap.

So-how long have you been taking sandbox?

I know what our sign says, Mrs. Bunyan, but even we are only equipped for the average exceptionally tall.

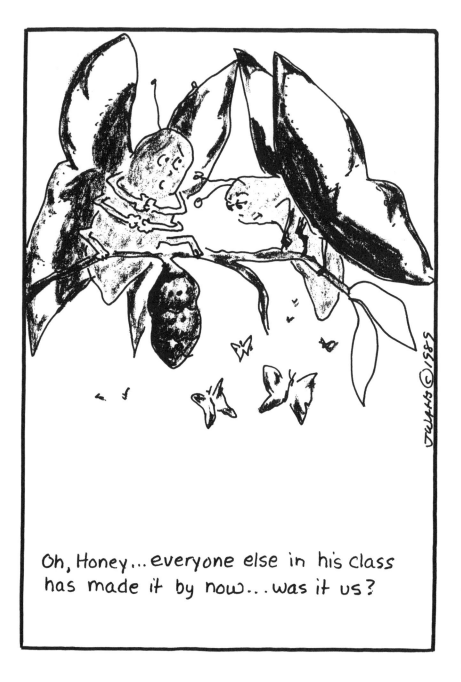

Oh, Honey... everyone else in his class
has made it by now... was it us?

It's disgusting how you children waste yourselves in front of that fire all day long... why — back in my day we never had fire and...

It's not that bad. I find I'm able to be self-actualized from 11 to 11:15 nearly every evening now.

My mother said teaching "divided we fall" is not fair to amoebas.

Yep... given the prodigy genes I've seen on these tests... I'd say your job as parents is essentially over!

It's not where we're headed, but the lack of solitude that bothers me the most.

It's Monday. Let me put my coat down first.

Oh, we had a great program last year
but she moved.

Write faster... I think that's technology going by us.

This is it. The test that will prove genius is detectable in a person's genes. From now on IQ tests and performance in life are obsolete.

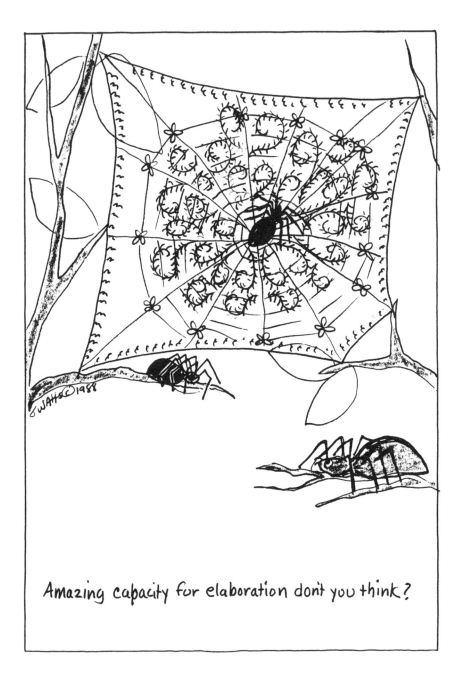

Amazing capacity for elaboration don't you think?

No sir... see right there it says I'm 3 !

Say—this teamwork stuff is great!

We were just deepening and broadening our capacity for self-disclosure, sir.

You have to admit - she's clear if nothing else.

Well, Casey, I'd say you would have
a fighting chance this time if grades were
drawn by lottery.

I'm going to rip you limb from limb, tear out your toenails, boil you in oil, and then you will go BACK to your seat and STAY there.

Sell the IBM, but wait until it hits 190, then,
about the Digital...wait, my parents are
home... "He DIDN'T!!... like WOW!...really COOL".

Well, the main idea is to keep me at my desk, right?

Oh, wait a minute, that said, "ask clarifying questions," not horrifying questions.

That's ok... I was just listening to a documentary about drag racing, but I've got it on pause.

Some of us are not in as big a rush to emerge.

What do you think? Should we believe
her or the evening news?

Oh no,..., it's the textbook salespeople—
they've found our committee !!

Well, actually, we have already initiated
a program for selecting the best, and most
pure students ...

Oh yes, in addition to acceleration,
we strive for depth.